How to Use

Each topic in this book contains the same four components. Use all four parts or customize the lessons to the needs of your students. After students have had some experience with the lessons, you may choose to place them in a center.

1

How to Draw a...
Each topic begins with a chart.

Post the chart in a center or make an overhead transparency to use as you guide students step by step through the drawing lesson.

2

Follow the Steps to Draw...
Step-by-step directions and a drawing space are provided for each topic.

3

Draw More...
Three variations on the topic are provided along with a drawing space.

4

Draw...Then Write About...
This reproducible form provides space for an original drawing of the subject, accompanied by directions for writing a paragraph about the drawing.

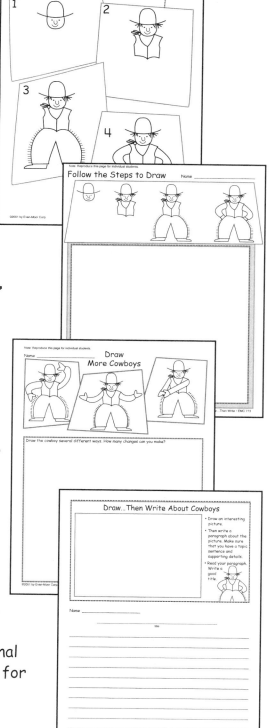

How to Draw a Dog

Draw…Then Write • EMC 773

Follow the Steps to Draw

Name _____

Name _____

Draw
More Dogs

Draw the dog several different ways. How many changes can you make?

Draw...Then Write About Dogs

- Draw an interesting picture.
- Then write a paragraph about the picture. Make sure that you have a topic sentence and supporting details.
- Read your paragraph. Write a good title.

Name _____

_____
title

_____

_____

_____

_____

_____

_____

_____

_____

How to Draw a Horse

Follow the Steps to Draw

Name _____

Name _____

Draw
More Horses

Draw the horse several different ways. How many changes can you make?

Draw...Then Write About Horses

- Draw an interesting picture.

- Then write a paragraph about the picture. Make sure that you have a topic sentence and supporting details.

- Read your paragraph. Write a good title.

Name _____

_____
title

_____

_____

_____

_____

_____

_____

_____

_____

_____

How to Draw a Cowboy

10

Follow the Steps to Draw

Name _____

Name _____

Draw
More Cowboys

Draw the cowboy several different ways. How many changes can you make?

Draw...Then Write About Cowboys

- Draw an interesting picture.

- Then write a paragraph about the picture. Make sure that you have a topic sentence and supporting details.

- Read your paragraph. Write a good title.

Name _____

_____
title

_____

_____

_____

_____

_____

_____

_____

_____

_____

_____

How to Draw a Cat

Follow the Steps to Draw

Name _____

Name _____

Draw
More Cats

Draw the cat several different ways. How many changes can you make?

Draw...Then Write About Cats

- Draw an interesting picture.
- Then write a paragraph about the picture. Make sure that you have a topic sentence and supporting details.
- Read your paragraph. Write a good title.

Name _____

_____
title

_____

_____

_____

_____

_____

_____

_____

_____

How to Draw an Elephant

Follow the Steps to Draw

Name _____

Name _____

Draw
More Elephants

Draw the elephant several different ways. How many changes can you make?

Draw...Then Write About Elephants

- Draw an interesting picture.
- Then write a paragraph about the picture. Make sure that you have a topic sentence and supporting details.
- Read your paragraph. Write a good title.

Name _____

_____
title

_____

_____

_____

_____

_____

_____

_____

_____

How to Draw an Astronaut

Follow the Steps to Draw

Name _____

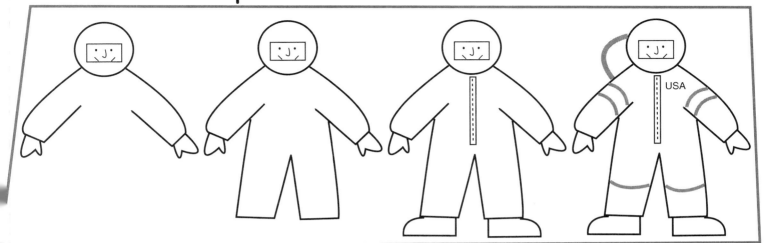

Name _____

Draw
More Astronauts

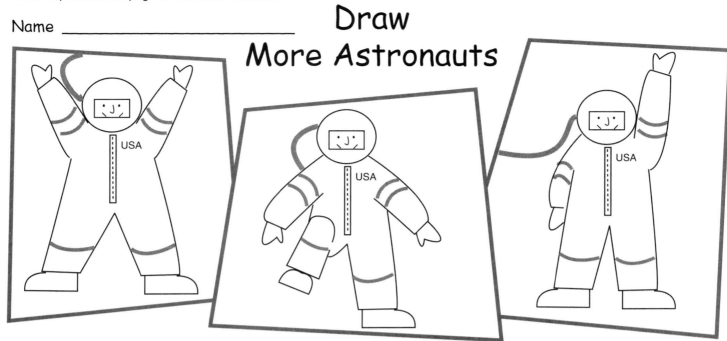

Draw the astronaut several different ways. How many changes can you make?

Draw...Then Write About Astronauts

- Draw an interesting picture.

- Then write a paragraph about the picture. Make sure that you have a topic sentence and supporting details.

- Read your paragraph. Write a good title.

USA

Name _____

_____
title

_____

_____

_____

_____

_____

_____

_____

_____

How to Draw a Pig

Follow the Steps to Draw

Name _____

Name _____

Draw More Pigs

Draw the pig several different ways. How many changes can you make?

Draw...Then Write About Pigs

- Draw an interesting picture.

- Then write a paragraph about the picture. Make sure that you have a topic sentence and supporting details.

- Read your paragraph. Write a good title.

Name _____

_____
title

_____

_____

_____

_____

_____

_____

_____

_____

_____

_____

How to Draw a Camel

Draw…Then Write • EMC 773

Follow the Steps to Draw

Name _____

Draw…Then Write • EMC 773

Name _____

Draw
More Camels

Draw the camel several different ways. How many changes can you make?

Draw...Then Write About Camels

- Draw an interesting picture.

- Then write a paragraph about the picture. Make sure that you have a topic sentence and supporting details.

- Read your paragraph. Write a good title.

Name _____

_____
title

_____

_____

_____

_____

_____

_____

_____

How to Draw a Football Player

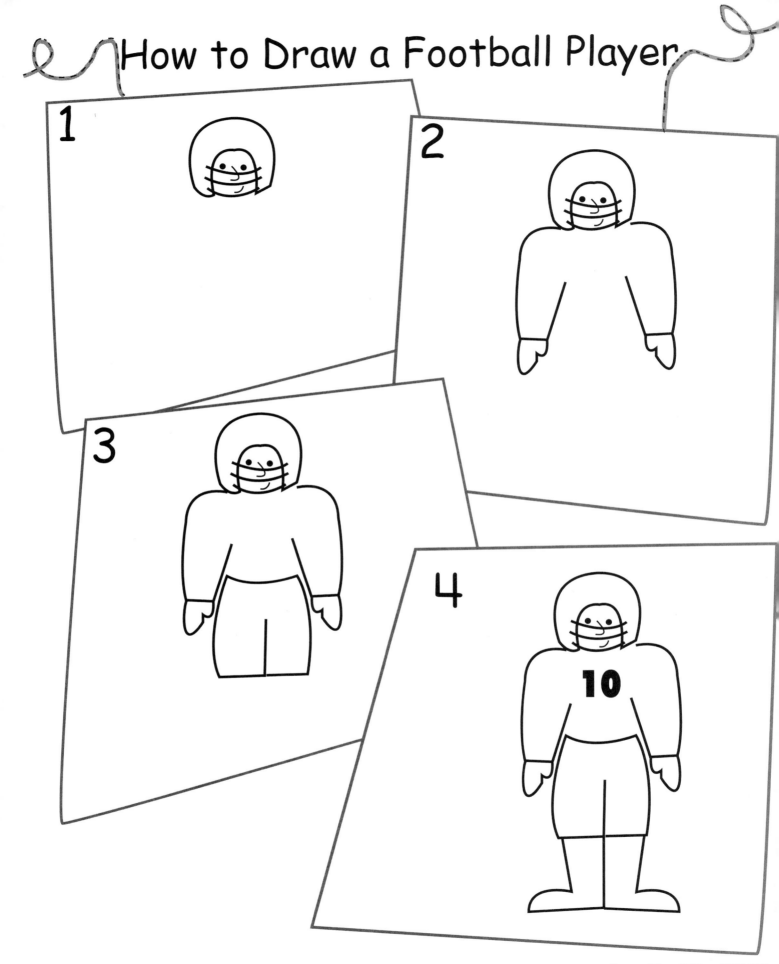

1

2

3

4

10

Draw…Then Write • EMC 773

Follow the Steps to Draw

Name _____

 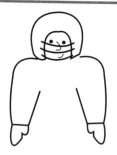  

Name _____

Draw
More Football Players

Draw the football player several different ways. How many changes can you make?

Draw...Then Write About a Football Player

- Draw an interesting picture.

- Then write a paragraph about the picture. Make sure that you have a topic sentence and supporting details.

- Read your paragraph. Write a good title.

10

Name _____

_____
title

_____

_____

_____

_____

_____

_____

_____

_____

_____

How to Draw a Knight

Follow the Steps to Draw

Name _____

Name _____

Draw
More Knights

Draw the knight several different ways. How many changes can you make?

40

Draw...Then Write About a Knight

- Draw an interesting picture.

- Then write a paragraph about the picture. Make sure that you have a topic sentence and supporting details.

- Read your paragraph. Write a good title.

Name _____

_____
title

_____

_____

_____

_____

_____

_____

_____

_____

_____

_____

How to Draw a Convertible

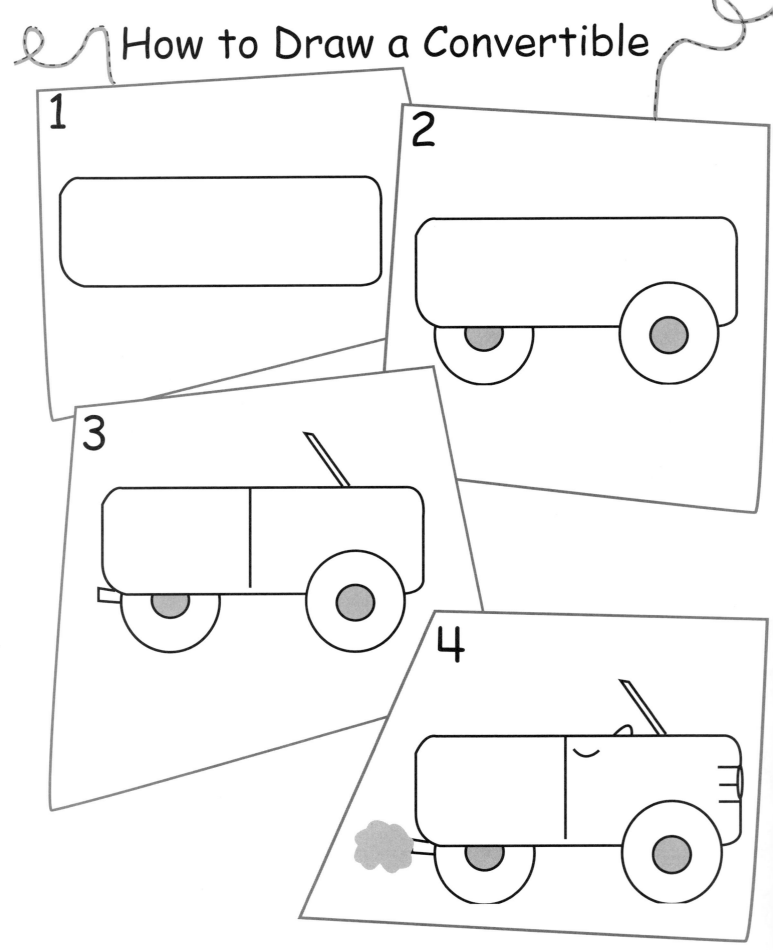

Follow the Steps to Draw

Name _____

Name _____

Draw More Convertibles

Draw the convertible several different ways. How many changes can you make?

44

Draw...Then Write About Your Convertible

- Draw an interesting picture.

- Then write a paragraph about the picture. Make sure that you have a topic sentence and supporting details.

- Read your paragraph. Write a good title.

Name _____

_____
title

How to Draw a Kangaroo

Follow the Steps to Draw

Name _____

Name _____

Draw
More Kangaroos

Draw the kangaroo several different ways. How many changes can you make?

Draw...Then Write About Kangaroos

- Draw an interesting picture.

- Then write a paragraph about the picture. Make sure that you have a topic sentence and supporting details.

- Read your paragraph. Write a good title.

Name _____

_____
title

_____

_____

_____

_____

_____

_____

_____

_____

How to Draw a Pirate

Follow the Steps to Draw

Name _____

Name _____

Draw
More Pirates

Draw the pirate several different ways. How many changes can you make?

Draw...Then Write About Pirates

- Draw an interesting picture.

- Then write a paragraph about the picture. Make sure that you have a topic sentence and supporting details.

- Read your paragraph. Write a good title.

Name _____

_____
title

_____

_____

_____

_____

_____

_____

_____

_____

How to Draw a Frog

Draw…Then Write • EMC 773

Follow the Steps to Draw

Name _____

Name _____

Draw
More Frogs

Draw the frog several different ways. How many changes can you make?

Draw...Then Write About Frogs

- Draw an interesting picture.

- Then write a paragraph about the picture. Make sure that you have a topic sentence and supporting details.

- Read your paragraph. Write a good title.

Name _____

_____
title

_____

_____

_____

_____

_____

_____

_____

_____

How to Draw a Gorilla

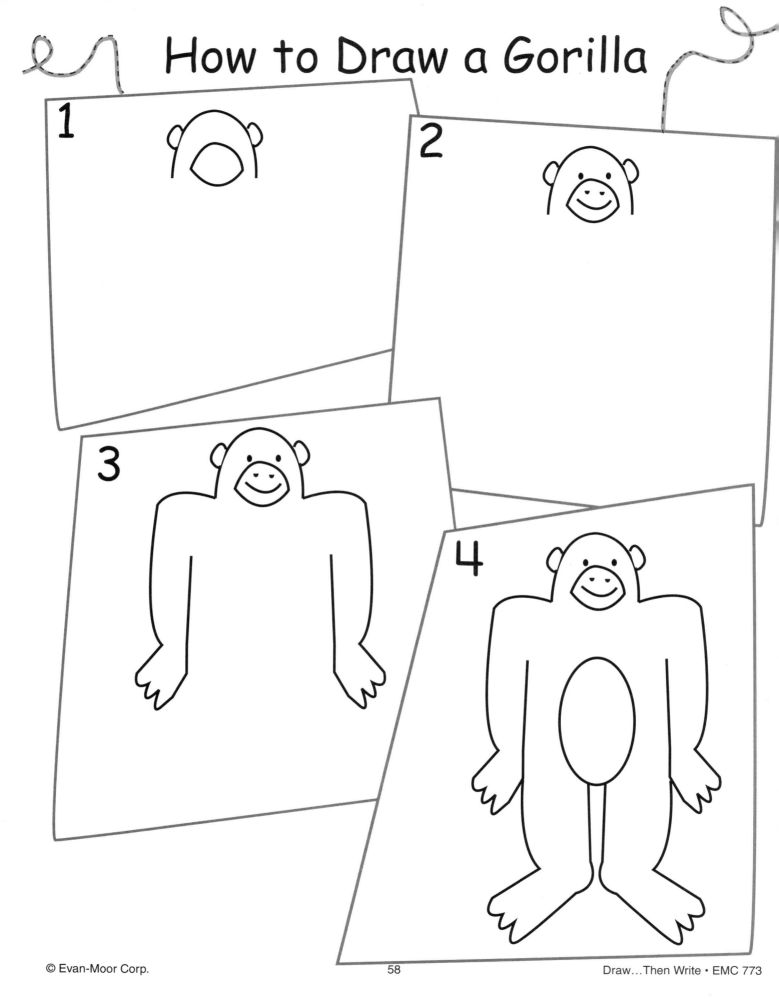

1

2

3

4

Draw…Then Write • EMC 773

Follow the Steps to Draw

Name _____

  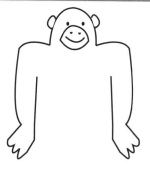 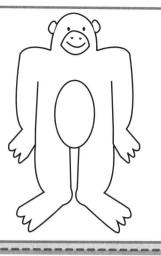

Name _____

Draw
More Gorillas

Draw the gorilla several different ways. How many changes can you make?

Draw...Then Write About Gorillas

- Draw an interesting picture.

- Then write a paragraph about the picture. Make sure that you have a topic sentence and supporting details.

- Read your paragraph. Write a good title.

Name _____

_____
title

_____

_____

_____

_____

_____

_____

_____

_____

_____

_____

How to Draw a Cheerleader

Follow the Steps to Draw

Name _____

Draw…Then Write • EMC 773

Name _____

Draw
More Cheerleaders

Draw the cheerleader several different ways. How many changes can you make?

Draw...Then Write About a Cheerleader

- Draw an interesting picture.

- Then write a paragraph about the picture. Make sure that you have a topic sentence and supporting details.

- Read your paragraph. Write a good title.

Name _____

_____
title

_____

_____

_____

_____

_____

_____

_____

_____

How to Draw a Bear

Follow the Steps to Draw

Name _____

Name _____

Draw
More Bears

Draw the bear several different ways. How many changes can you make?

Draw...Then Write About Bears

- Draw an interesting picture.
- Then write a paragraph about the picture. Make sure that you have a topic sentence and supporting details.
- Read your paragraph. Write a good title.

Name _____

_____
title

_____

_____

_____

_____

_____

_____

_____

_____

How to Draw a Crocodile

Follow the Steps to Draw

Name _____

  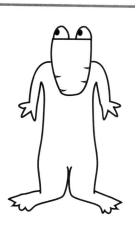 

Name _____

Draw
More Crocodiles

Draw the crocodiles several different ways. How many changes can you make?

Draw...Then Write About Crocodiles

- Draw an interesting picture.

- Then write a paragraph about the picture. Make sure that you have a topic sentence and supporting details.

- Read your paragraph. Write a good title.

Name _____

_____

title

_____

_____

_____

_____

_____

_____

_____

_____

_____

_____

How to Draw a Skater

Follow the Steps to Draw

Name _____

Name _____

Draw
More Skaters

Draw the skaters several different ways. How many changes can you make?

Draw...Then Write About a Skater

- Draw an interesting picture.

- Then write a paragraph about the picture. Make sure that you have a topic sentence and supporting details.

- Read your paragraph. Write a good title.

Name _____

_____
title

_____

_____

_____

_____

_____

_____

_____

_____

How to Draw a Penguin

78

Follow the Steps to Draw

Name _____

Name _____

Draw
More Penguins

Draw the penguin several different ways. How many changes can you make?

Draw...Then Write About Penguins

- Draw an interesting picture.

- Then write a paragraph about the picture. Make sure that you have a topic sentence and supporting details.

- Read your paragraph. Write a good title.

Name _____

_____
title

_____

_____

_____

_____

_____

_____

_____

_____

How to Draw a Rider on a Scooter

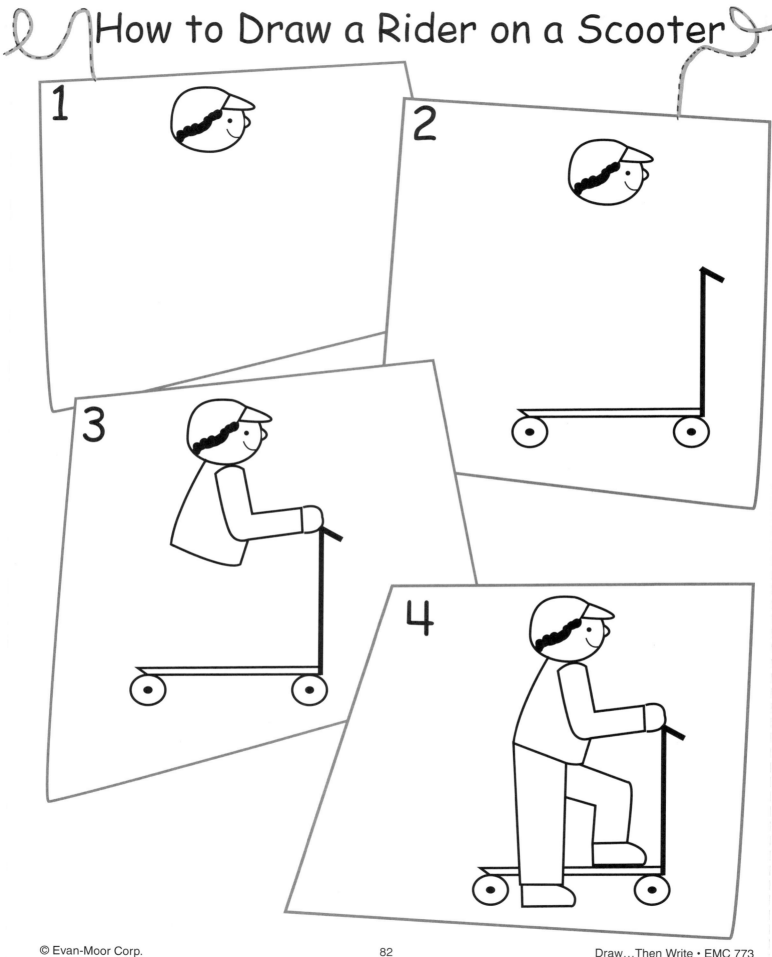

Follow the Steps to Draw

Name _____

Name _____

Draw
More Scooter Riders

Draw the scooter rider several different ways. How many changes can you make?

Draw...Then Write About a Scooter Rider

- Draw an interesting picture.

- Then write a paragraph about the picture. Make sure that you have a topic sentence and supporting details.

- Read your paragraph. Write a good title.

Name _____

_____
title

_____
_____
_____
_____
_____
_____
_____
_____
_____
_____

How to Draw a Bird

Follow the Steps to Draw

Name _____

Name _____

Draw
More Birds

Draw the bird several different ways. How many changes can you make?

Draw...Then Write • EMC 773

Draw...Then Write About Birds

- Draw an interesting picture.

- Then write a paragraph about the picture. Make sure that you have a topic sentence and supporting details.

- Read your paragraph. Write a good title.

Name _____

_____
title

How to Draw a Hippo

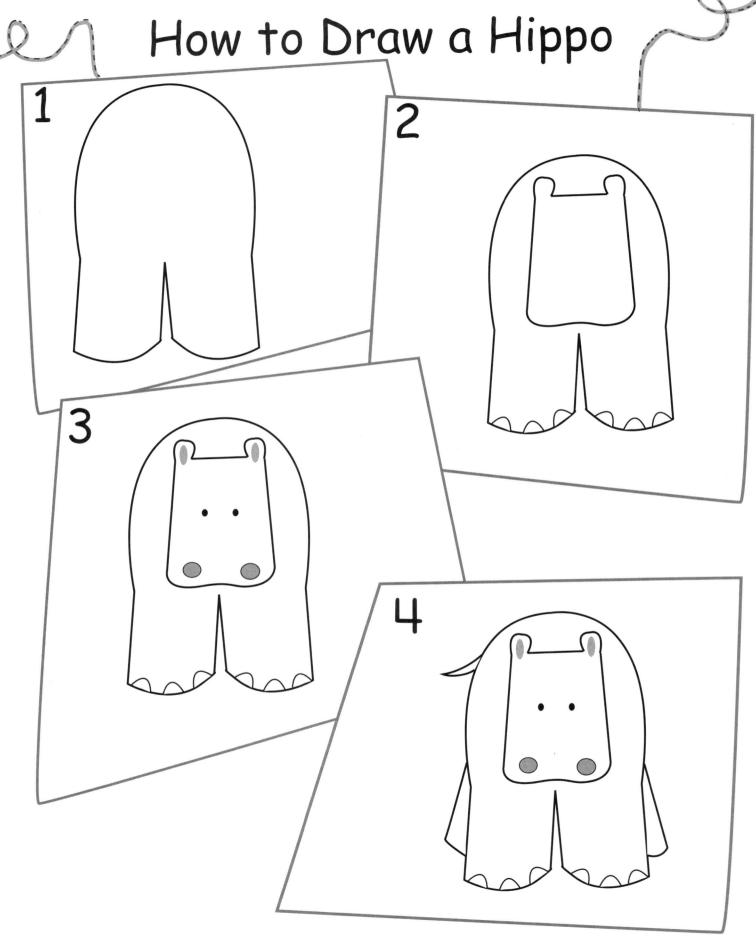

Follow the Steps to Draw

Name _____

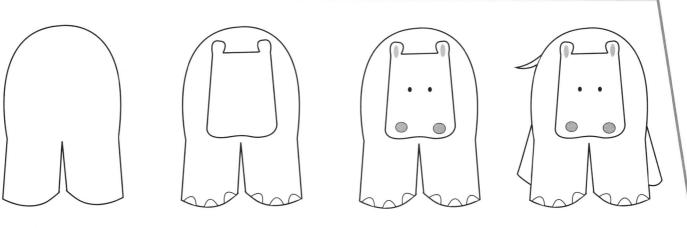

Name _____

Draw
More Hippos

Draw the hippo several different ways. How many changes can you make?

Draw...Then Write About Hippos

- Draw an interesting picture.

- Then write a paragraph about the picture. Make sure that you have a topic sentence and supporting details.

- Read your paragraph. Write a good title.

Name _____

_____
title

_____

_____

_____

_____

_____

_____

_____

_____

_____

Backgrounds for Your Drawings

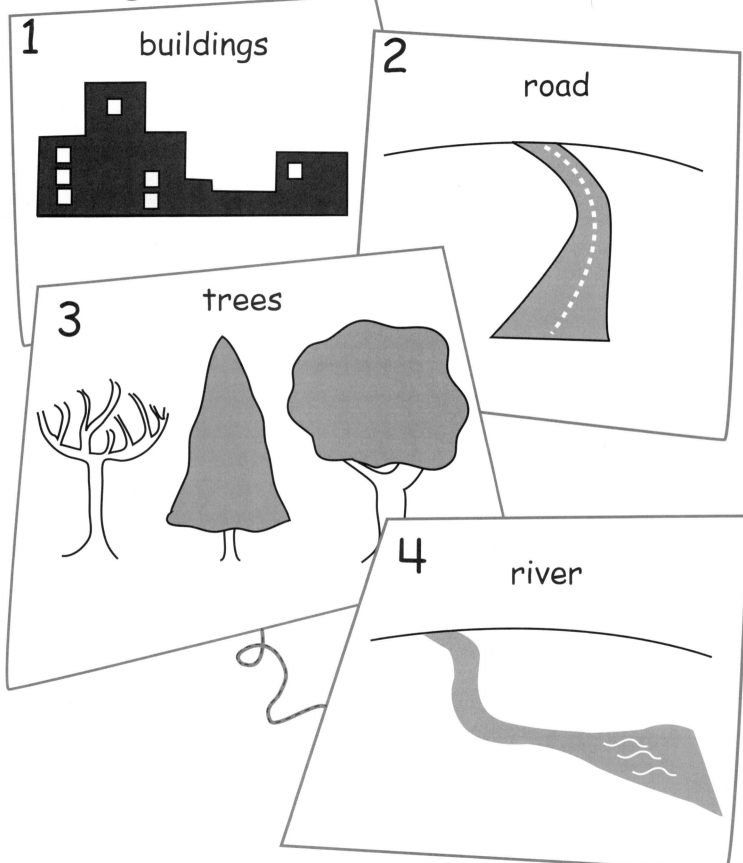

1 buildings

2 road

3 trees

4 river

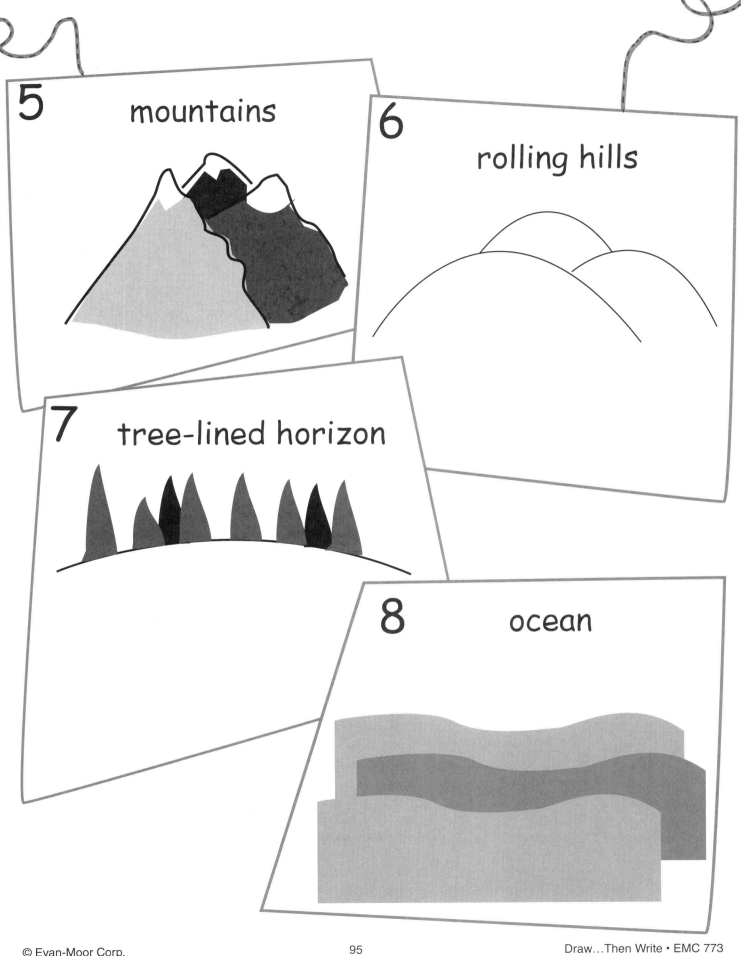

5 mountains

6 rolling hills

7 tree-lined horizon

8 ocean

Draw…Then Write • EMC 773

Note: Reproduce these lines for students to use for longer stories.

More Draw...Then Write